The Swell

Isley Lynn

T0284388

methuen | drama

LONDON · NEW YORK · OXFORD · NEW DELHI · SYDNEY

METHUEN DRAMA
Bloomsbury Publishing Plc
50 Bedford Square, London, WC1B 3DP, UK
1385 Broadway, New York, NY 10018, USA
29 Earlsfort Terrace, Dublin 2, Ireland

BLOOMSBURY, METHUEN DRAMA and the Methuen
Drama logo are trademarks of Bloomsbury Publishing Plc

First published in Great Britain 2023

A catalogue record for this book is available from the British Library.

A catalog record for this book is available from the Library of Congress.

ISBN: PB: 978-1-3504-3883-5
ePDF: 978-1-3504-3884-2
eBook: 978-1-3504-3885-9

Series: Modern Plays

Typeset by Mark Heslington Ltd, Scarborough, North Yorkshire

To find out more about our authors and books visit
www.bloomsbury.com and sign up for our newsletters.

THE SWELL
24 June–29 July 2023

An Orange Tree Theatre co-production with Damsel Productions and The Women's Prize for Playwriting

Cast

Bel	**Ruby Crepin-Glyne**
Annie	**Saroja-Lily Ratnavel**
Flo	**Jessica Clark**
B	**Sophie Ward**
F	**Shuna Snow**
A	**Viss Elliot Safavi**

Writer   Isley Lynn
Director   Hannah Hauer-King
Designer   Amy Jane Cook
Lighting Designer   Elliot Griggs
Sound Designer, Composer & Co-Musical Director   Nicola T Chang
Co-Musical Director   Sinéad Rodger
Assistant Director   Sam Woof
Casting Consultant   Polly Jerrold
Fight & Intimacy Director   Bethan Clark
Production Manager   Stuart Burgess
Company Stage Manager   Jenny Skivens
Deputy Stage Manager   Sussan Sanii
Assistant Stage Manager   Laura Dewhirst

A powerhouse of independent theatre

The Orange Tree (OT) is an award-winning, independent theatre. Recognised as a powerhouse that creates high-quality productions of new and rediscovered plays, we entertain 70,000 people across the UK every year.

The OT's home in Richmond, South West London, is an intimate theatre with the audience seated all around the stage: watching a performance here is truly a unique experience.

We believe in the power of dramatic stories to entertain, thrill and challenge us; plays that enrich our lives by enhancing our understanding of ourselves and each other.

As a registered charity (266128) sitting at the heart of its community, we work with 10,000 people in Richmond and beyond through participatory theatre projects for everyone.

The Orange Tree Theatre's mission is to enable audiences to experience the next generation of theatre talent, experiment with ground-breaking new drama and explore the plays from the past that inspire the theatre-makers of the present. To find out how you can help us to do that you can visit **orangetreetheatre.co.uk/support-us**

orangetreetheatre.co.uk

Registered charity no. 266128

DAMSEL
PRODUCTIONS

Hannah Hauer-King and Kitty Wordsworth co-founded theatre company Damsel Productions in 2015 to produce hit show *Dry Land* at Jermyn Street Theatre. Since then, Damsel has continued to produce work with the core aim of developing and platforming scripts written by women, and produced with primarily women-led creative teams.

Damsel has produced several full-scale productions at theatres including Soho Theatre, Theatre 503, the Bunker Theatre and Jermyn Street Theatre.

They have also produced sell-out live comedy and cabaret nights such as *Damsel In The Bush;* and festivals including *Damsel Develops*, London's first all-women directing festival; and *Damsel Outdoors*, a festival of commissioned new plays written for the outdoors during the pandemic.

The Swell is their first production at the Orange Tree Theatre.

Damselproductions.co.uk

   @DamselProd
@damselproductions

Founded by Ellie Keel and Paines Plough in 2019, the Women's Prize for Playwriting is one step in the movement towards redressing the gender balance of plays produced in our theatres. By seeking out, championing and staging extraordinary new plays by women, we hope to redefine and revitalise the canon for future generations. We work with a judging panel of exceptional leaders in their field to award a cash prize of £12,000 to the winning playwright and produce their play on a major stage in the UK or Ireland.

Most recently, *Reasons You Should(n't) Love Me* by Amy Trigg has had a smash-hit run at Kiln Theatre and on tour throughout the UK, and been produced for audio by Audible, and *You Bury Me* by Ahlam has had a major, critically-acclaimed tour to Bristol Old Vic, the Royal Lyceum Theatre, Edinburgh, and the Orange Tree Theatre in London.

Find out more: **www.womensprizeforplaywriting.co.uk**.

Judging Panel 2023: Samira Ahmed, April de Angelis, Chris Bush, Noma Dumezweni, Mel Kenyon, Indhu Rubasingham (Chair), Anya Ryan, Nina Steiger, Katharine Viner.

We are exceptionally grateful to our **Advisory** Council for their support and expertise: Rosie Allison, Kate Ashton, Kathleen Bacon (Chair), Rupert Gavin, Daisy Goodwin, Aidan Grounds, Raxita Kapashi, Tessa Murray.

THE TEAM

Founder Director Ellie Keel

Ellie studied Modern Languages at Oxford University and developed a successful career as an theatre producer before founding the Women's Prize for Playwriting in 2019. She launched the prize with Founding Partner, Paines Plough, after a litany of unacceptable statistics made it clear that plays by women writers were severely underrepresented on national stages in the UK and Ireland.

As Founder Director, Ellie leads on all aspects of strategy, communications and fundraising for the Women's Prize for Playwriting, as well as overseeing the day-to-day operations and administration of the Prize. With Paines Plough, Ellie is also responsible for programming and co-producing plays which win the Women's Prize for Playwriting, and for championing the plays which reach the longlist, shortlist and finalist stages.

Her credits include the sell-out shows *HOTTER* and *FITTER* by Mary Higgins and Ell Potter (Soho Theatre, Traverse Theatre and tour; *Reasons You Should(n't) Love Me* by Amy Trigg (Kiln Theatre, Audible and tour); the multi award-winning *Sap* by Rafaella Marcus (Roundabout, Soho Theatre and tour); *Collapsible* by Margaret Perry (Bush Theatre, HighTide Festival, Abbey Theatre and tour); and *Redefining Juliet* (Barbican Centre).

Ellie is also a writer and her first novel, *THE FOUR*, will be published by HarperCollins in April 2024.

Literary Associate Tommo Fowler

Tommo is a Sheffield-based dramaturg for text and production, and a director.

As Literary Associate, he oversees writers' submissions, coordinates the hiring and training of readers, and facilitates the reading process for entries to the Prize – as well as supporting its strategic development.

He is co-founder of award-winning dramaturgy company RoughHewn (Olwen Wymark Award, Writers' Guild of Great Britain), a Board Member of the Dramaturgs' Network, and a reader for BBC Writersroom.

He was Residencies Dramaturg and a Supported Artist at Sheffield Theatres, and has also been a reader for multiple theatres and awards, including the Royal Court, Traverse, Bush Theatre and Bruntwood Prize. He was previously Visiting Tutor on the MA Playwriting at City, University of London, and has run dramaturgy seminars and workshops for Leeds Conservatoire, Rose Bruford, Extant and Lyric Theatre Belfast.

As a dramaturg, theatre includes *Jews. In Their Own Words.* (Royal Court), *One Jewish Boy* (Trafalgar Studios), *Out of the Dark* (Rose Theatre Kingston), *There Is No Planet B* (Theatre Deli, Sheffield) and *In My Lungs the Ocean Swells* (VAULT Festival, Origins Award).

As a director, theatre includes *Stray Dogs* (Theatre503), *Jam, I Wish To Die Singing, Obama-ology* (Finborough Theatre), *How to make a revolution* (Finborough Online), *Comet* (Pleasance, Islington), *Mumburger* (Old Red Lion), *Boy* (Leeds Conservatoire), *The Strip, Fear* and *Misery of the Third Reich* (Oxford School of Drama).

 **@WomensPlayPrize**

Writer's Note

I found it so difficult to write this. Not the play – which has been in my brain for sixteen years, and poured out of me over a single week in 2018 – but the writer's note. It's so difficult to talk about this play without spoiling it in some way; either by steering your impressions of the characters, or giving away the ending, or diminishing the room it holds for multiple responses and reactions, all of which are valid. So instead, I thought I'd take this chance to list all the things that are in the play that you might not otherwise know were there:

The film my friend told me would be the saddest thing I would ever see – as I watched the film, I thought I saw a devastating end coming, but that ending didn't happen. I was disappointed, but I had an idea for a new play.

My short play for LOST Theatre's 5 Min Fest in 2012, directed by Amanda Castro.

The generosity of the actors in the 2017 HighTide First Commissions workshop.

The gentleness and tenacity of Hannah Hauer-King and Jonathan Kinnersley.

Jess and Shuna's un-pierced ears.

The diaries of Anaïs Nin.

The song 'You and Me on the Rock' by Brandi Carlisle.

Oliver Sacks' book *The Man Who Mistook His Wife for a Hat*.

The Harvard study that's referenced in the play.

Every true crime documentary I've seen about spies and kidnapping and men with secret families.

YouTube videos of people after their wisdom teeth are taken out.

The work of Verity Standen.

Always getting my name spelled wrong in Starbucks.

People who complain about historical figures being played by actors who don't look like them.

Returning to the town I grew up in and finding that all the shops had changed.

Geoffrey, who told me his heart was swelling.

My exes, who were quick to apologise but couldn't change.

Sarah Kosar's radical beautiful life pivot.

Another friend's decision to make it so that his sister didn't know she was cut from their inheritance for being a lesbian.

Rob and Sarah's place in Wales.

Barry's place in Box Hill.

The language that Hollie Rogers and I share, which is 80 per cent in-jokes.

Hollie's ex's sister's brain.

Everyone who ever dragged me onto a dance floor when I really didn't want to dance.

All the women I love and have loved and could love and will love.

Everyone who's known I loved them and has given me the gift of not being weird about it.

Blythe Stewart teaching me yoga.

My dad being so bad at yoga.

My brother hearing the song in everything.

My mom's career as an opera singer, then a speech and language therapist.

My mom's story of getting her ears pierced.

My grandmother's stroke.

My grandmother's subsequent prosopagnosia, meaning she no longer recognised me.

The poem I wrote about this, included below.

The little lies we told my grandmother in order to calm her down when her brain could no longer stop an anxiety spiral.

My mother caring for my grandmother, and everyone else around her.

My aunt's sudden death, during the first week of rehearsals.

The final tweaks and trims with Hannah and the gorgeous cast that are happening as I write this note.

So much of writing isn't about putting words on a page. And so much of these pages I owe to others. Thanks so much, all.

The body but hides the heart
(a letter to my grandmother after her stroke)

Please
I beg you
Do not feel guilt
For forgetting the way my figure is built
For I am no tall, redheaded girl
With pale skin or dark eyes
I am only your granddaughter
This body but hides the heart inside
Which you have filled with love
And my face is for nothing but to show it
My lips but to speak it
My hands but to hold yours
My arms but to take you in them
My skin but to feel you
My ears but to hear you
My eyes but to see you
And if they are glossy and filling with tears
It is with such thanks that we've kept what's most dear
Not our meat, our bones, our organs and blood
But our love
So care not who enters
See not their stuff
If they tell you they love you
That's enough

Thanks to

Robyn Keynes, Roy Alexander-Weise and Steven Atkinson.
Amanda Castro, Duncan Joyce and Dashiel Munding. Tom Littler,
Taj Atwal, Syreeta Kumar, Flora Montgomery, Sophie Harkness,
Jess Clark, Shuna Snow, Komal Amin, Libby Rodliffe, Blythe
Stewart and Hannah Hauer-King. Stevie Hopwood and fellow
Crowtherers Jennifer Claessen and Alan Ward. Vinay Patel and
fellow Playdaters Sarah Kosar, David Ralf, Christopher Adams,
Stephen Laughton and Poppy Corbett. Defectors Kelly Jones,
Afsaneh Gray, Tom Wentworth and Robyn Addison. Plant Bangers
Amalia Vitale, Roberta Zuric, Emma Waterford and Kat Bond (and
Libby and Jess). Jonathan Kinnersley. Geoffrey Stuart. My family.

The Swell

for Mom

And they say that the truth will set you free
But then so will a lie

> – Ani DiFranco, 'Promised Land'

I know love is a stranger
I know that changes come
I know love is a changer

> – Anais Mitchell, 'Changer'

'So it's not gonna be easy. It's going to be really
hard; we're gonna have to work at this everyday,
but I want to do that because I want you. I want
all of you, forever, everyday. You and me . . .
everyday.'

> – Nicholas Sparks, *The Notebook*

Characters

Bel, *twenties*
Annie, *twenty-seven*
Flo, *twenty-nine*

Then twenty-eight years pass

B
F
A

Notes

/ marks the point of interruption in overlapping dialogue
If a character's line ends with – and their next lines begins with –
then the lines run on as one without pause
[ ] indicates speech which is not said out loud but is included to
clarify the intention of the line

A phone is ringing, unanswered.

B (*calling*)   Flo. Flo. Flooooo. Flo!

F   What!

B   The phone!

F   I know.

B   Are we not going to answer it?

F   Who's going to be calling us?

B   Someone's sold our number?

F   Definitely. It'll just be a robot.

B   It's the online shopping.

F   I'm not talking about that again, Bel, it's necessary.

The phone stops ringing.

F *acknowledges this with a gesture.*

B   Flo?

F   Bel.

B   Are these my glasses?

F   Yes.

B looks at the spectacles in her hand.

*F sees this hesitation and takes them from her,
placing them on her face for her, not impatient.*

B thanks her physically somehow, something small.

F   Bad day?

B   Yeah.

F   I'll join you in the bath. Do your hair.

B   That would be really nice.

A LARGE, EXCITED GASP

Flo *and* **Annie** *are embracing, joyful noises.*

Annie   It's so so good to see you.

Flo   It's so good to see you! (*To* **Bel**.) And you! It's great to meet you.

Annie   Bel, this is Flo.

Bel   I've heard so much about you.

Flo   You are exactly what I thought you would be.

Bel   Oh yeah?

Flo   No, not at all.

They laugh.

Flo   You are – no, you're not anything like I imagined.

Bel   What did you imagine?

Annie   How long are you here?

Flo   Till the wedding! And then you know me, no firm anything, just thought I'd come.

Annie   No, no, Flo, not this year next year.

Flo   What?

Annie   The wedding –

Flo   'Wedding'!

Annie   – is next year, Flo.

Flo   I'm not an idiot I can read, I know it's / next year.

Annie   Oh, so you're staying that whole time?

Flo Yes!

Annie Aren't you – don't you / have . . .

Flo Not with you, don't worry, I'll find a place, no this is just for as long as that takes.

Annie Right.

Flo I thought to myself, it was just a wake-up call that you know life is going on without me. Because I had no idea about all this, and like how did I not know this was happening. So I'm coming back, I'm done being a nomad. I'm putting down roots. (*Winking.*) At least for a bit.

Annie I'll believe that when I see it.

Flo You'll see it.

Bel Is that because of the surfing? Your surfing?

Flo Right, exactly. See she gets it.

Bel Can I help you with your – that bag is huge.

Flo I'm used to it, don't worry.

Bel Well, Anais, maybe you can bring the car around so / we don't have to . . .

Flo Ooh 'Anais'.

Annie That's my name.

Flo But it's so weird to hear someone say it correctly.

Annie She's my fiancée, she ought / to know my name.

Flo I know I know I just, I'm just excited. (*To* **Bel**.) I get like this. And the journey! And now I'm here and I just want to know all about you! Everything. Fill me in on everything.

Annie Let's fill you in at home.

Flo No let's fill me in at a pub or something, somewhere with food, I haven't eaten yet, like Caffe Gemini?

Annie   Gemini is a boutique jewellery shop now.

Flo   Christ.

Annie   But there's loads of places to eat, you'll see, lots of coffee shops, sandwich shops. We'll have a swift something because I've / got things to do . . .

Flo   You know everyone's always getting her name wrong.

Bel   I know, I've seen. Even at her work / still . . .

Flo   You're very impressive.

Annie (*teasing*)   Why are you so surprised!

Flo (*to* **Bel**)   She used to really kick off about it.

Bel   Oh really?

Flo   Oh yeah.

Bel   You don't any more do you.

Annie   Annie's just easier, for everyone.

Bel   She's actually always saying, aren't you, saying, 'Well the name's not the thing is it'.

Annie   No. It's the person.

Bel (*sharing a loving smile*)   Yeah.

Flo   This got very gooey very fast, let's go. So, Bel. Is 'Bel' the whole thing with you?

Bel   No, short for Belinda.

Flo   Oh, so it's like Baby Bel not *Beauty and the Beast* Belle?

Bel   Uh, right. Is Flo short for Florence?

Flo   No, no. Emma.

B *and* **F** *are facing each other.*

F *is not taking this seriously.*

B So you're meant to do this to the sun. You're saying hello.

F The sun would have to arrive first.

B So we'll just do it to each other.

F Hello.

B Hello. So first you need to feel your feet. Feel yourself standing.

F I feel my feet I feel myself standing.

B Feel yourself rooted to the ground.

F I am rooted to the ground.

B And you're going to take a deep breath from inside.

F (*sarcastic*) Where else would it come from?

B Like it's coming from that root. It's not coming from your ribs it's deeper. It's coming from your toes.

F My toes.

B Your toes.

F Are breathing.

B Yes.

F Ok hold on here we go.

F deeply breathes in.

F Oh, it does actually feel – / If I . . .

B Yeah arsehole.

F If I just think about it coming from, hold on . . .

F breathes in again.

B That's good.

F That is good.

B   Just make that breath fill your whole body. And when you're ready you're going to relax your knees so that / everything is relaxed . . .

F   Bend my knees?

B   Yep so your knees are relaxed and flexible. And what we do is when we take a breath we dip a little and –

F dips too much, almost squats.

B   – with the arms we lift them above our head and inhale.

F struggles with this.

B   Flo, you should really be able to do that.

F   I'm doing it!

B   And when you exhale bring your hands to your heart.

They both do so.

B (*physically correcting her*)   So your heart is here, between your sternum, just a little bit higher.

F   So on top of my tits.

B   And then breathe out in ocean breath.

They do this together.

B   And then you bring them up again above your head . . .

B has only lifted her right arm fully up.

F   Arm.

B brings her left arm up.

B   Thank you. And your fingers are up, they're out to the world, stretch stretch stretch stretch, and on your exhale you drop to the ground, you don't have to touch the ground, your knees are still really bent.

F moans.

B   See you're so tight, remember to feel your feet.

F   I'm feeling my feet I'm feeling everything.

B   Ok and now the next part this might be a little complicated, we'll do a few things at once.

F   Tell me quick I can't hold this.

B   You're going to breathe in halfway.

F   What?

B   So you're going to breathe in and come halfway up to a table, / and you want to make it as flat as possible.

F   This is unnatural this is, is this really necessary?

B   It's not hurting you.

F   Yes it is.

B   You're not even doing it.

F stands.

B   Get back down there!

F does.

B   Just relax into it.

F bounces her arse up and down.

B   That's it, more like that.

F bounces more.

B pauses to stifle a laugh.

F   Don't laugh – are you taking the piss!

B   Only a little.

F (*standing*)   God you are, you're taking the piss! Look I don't *feel* stiff ok, I felt fine until all this.

B   I can see that you're stiff!

F   Well, I'm fine stiff! I'm happy stiff!

B   This is important because it will help, / it will help with everything –

   F *is breathing ocean breath loudly at* **B**, *mocking, silencing her.*

B   – That's really very good ocean breath, Flo, well done.

F   Thank you.

B   It's bound to help with surfing.

F   Oh yes *surfing, my surfing* . . .

B   Well, won't it?

Beat.

F   It's more like boogie boarding at this point.

B   Look this is what we're going to do.

F   I'm looking.

B (*demonstrating*)   You go into a plank.

F   No.

B (*demonstrating*)   Then you go into downward dog.

F   I see. Hold on.

   F *lies on the floor on her stomach with her torso stretched up.*

B (*joining her in position*)   Your belly has to be off the floor.

F   Fuck off.

B (*demonstrating cat pose*)   Ok let's do this instead . . .

F   Can we just stay here for a bit.

B   You'll like this.

B *demonstrates, breathing in and out as*
she arches her spine up and down.

F   Hold on, just leave me here.

B   It's easy, watch me.

B continues to demonstrate.

F watches with a smile.

F   One more time?

B arches one way . . .

F   You are . . .

. . . then the other.

F   . . . gorgeous, you know that? You are beautiful.

B   You are not taking this seriously.

F   I am very serious. You are seriously beautiful. Show me again, hold on . . .

*F lies on her back, positions herself underneath **B**'s face.*

F   Maybe I'll understand it better from this angle.

B   You arse. You arse arse arse.

They kiss.

B   I'm only doing this for you.

F (*insinuating*)   Let me repay you.

B   You know, if you don't stretch, soon you'll stop being able to make good on those offers.

F   But not yet.

HARD LAUGHTER, CATCHING BREATH

Flo   We were all getting them done, there was a whole group of us, it was someone's older sister – whose sister was it?

Annie   I don't know.

Flo   She was doing them with a needle, like really old school, that's how / we did it.

Annie   And an apple, she'd cut up an apple for the other / side, I mean how . . .

Flo   And you bottled it, you completely bottled it –

Annie   I / just didn't . . .

Flo   – and she just never has!

Annie   But all that blood, she had blood all in her fingernails / it was so . . .

Flo   But I turned out fine.

Annie   I can't do it, nope, it just gives me the – it makes me – urgh, no. Never.

Flo   Wuss.

Annie   I don't need to do it, I don't have to do it.

Flo (*reaching over and swiping an earring from her ear*)   But you clearly want to do it because you have / all these clip on ones –

Annie (*snatching the earring back, re-fixing it to her lobe*)   Flo!

Flo   – and you'd have much more range if you just . . .

Annie   Right! I can get the same thing the same effect without butchering myself!

Flo (*mocking*)   'Butchering yourself.'

Annie   It is butchery! / It is!

Flo (*to* **Bel**)   We're just going to talk in circles, you have to stop this, you, so, your turn. Story time.

Bel   I don't really have stories, any stories.

Flo   Sure you do. How you met, tell me how you met, I still don't know that, I don't know anything because (*to* **Annie**) you are a stone.

Annie (*to* **Bel**)   Do you want to tell it?

Bel   I think we should co-tell it.

Annie   That is the worst thing, everyone hates when couples do that.

Flo   No do it do it go on be gross you've earned it you deserve it you're getting married! Go on, be gross.

Annie   Ok ok, so, I, uh, was setting up the company at the time, across the street from the coffee shop.

Flo   A coffee shop, romantic, I love it already, keep going.

Annie   And Bel worked at the coffee shop. And I would go in there all the time.

Bel   She would be there at really odd times, like not the regular lunch and commute or anything, or at closing.

Annie   Yeah sometimes I would run over there just before they closed.

Bel   And I didn't know at the time it was because she was doing everything to start up the company.

Flo   This is your charity.

Annie   Non-profit.

Flo   She always was a goody goody.

Bel   She works so hard, she's always at work.

Annie   Most of the time she wasn't on the tills.

Bel   I would be making the drinks, and everyone does a bit of every job but I would most often be doing that because I was really fast at it. And I (*laughs*) one day this, stunning woman that comes in here all the time comes up and I happen to be on the till and she says her name.

Flo   Right, her weird name.

Annie   I say it as clearly as / possible because . . .

Flo   But don't you say Annie?

Annie   Yeah I would but, I think because she was taking my order and I wanted to impress her or something with my fancy name.

Flo   With your fucking fancy name.

Annie   Right, so I say 'Anais' and she –

Bel   And I, now I promise you, I hear 'anus'. And I think, why are you doing this? You're an arsehole, literally being an arsehole, and I was so disappointed like oh fuck ok she's not worth my time. So I was so mad I think that this person I had a massive crush on was being this mean, that I just I write 'ANUS' on the cup, like I call her bluff, which I absolutely should not have done even if someone did say anus, but I did. And then when her order is made she picks up the cup.

Annie   I pick up the cup and I see 'ANUS'.

Bel   She sees I've written 'ANUS' and she just starts laughing in a way which makes clear she wasn't, this wasn't what she was expecting to happen, it's not a prank, and I realise I've really fucked up I've really made a mistake.

Annie   This happens all the time but I've never had 'ANUS', I've had all sorts but not anus.

Bel   So anyway I apologise.

Annie   She apologises like twenty times, like twenty different ways.

Bel   And I give her a voucher for loads of money and anyway, that is that. Basically. After that point you came in the regular amount, used your voucher, I tried to make sure I took your order, or if I was making drinks I'd make sure I'd give it to you and we'd always, smile. And then you asked me out didn't you?

Annie   Yeah I did.

Flo   No! That is the most shocking part of this story – you asked her out!

Annie   Yeah.

Flo (*to* **Bel**)   And were you out at this point?

Bel   Uh, no.

Annie   Not until the –

Flo   Right. Incredible. So, so what, you just asked, what on a date?

Bel   Not explicitly a date but it was heavily implied. To anyone with, anyone basically. So then we went on a date that wasn't a date but was definitely a date.

Flo   Wow. Ok. That is, like it's not spectacular but it's pretty cute. (*To* **Bel**.) And then how long were you together before you proposed.

Annie   I did that as well.

Flo   You proposed! What's going on – who are you – what have you done with my friend Annie!

Annie   It was about half a year.

Flo   Half a year. Wow. Ok. That's fast.

Annie   It doesn't feel fast, it doesn't, what's going to / happen that I don't already know, you know . . .

Bel   Actually – sorry, sorry – that's a story too.

Annie   Oh no.

Bel   No it's sweet it's funny.

Flo   I am already extremely excited for this.

Annie   / It's –

Bel   Tell her.

Annie   No . . .

Bel   She said to me . . . You're really not going to [tell her]?

Annie   I said . . . (*rolling her eyes, with love*) I said. My heart is swelling.

Flo   Sorry what?

Bel   I thought she was terminally ill!

Flo is laughing and laughing.

Annie   It was heartfelt!

Bel   It was, I loved it, once you explained what you meant.

Annie   Alright, Flo, it's not / stand-up it's sincere ok.

Bel   She goes 'For you! For you!'

Flo   That is the best, gayest thing I've ever heard.

Annie can't help but laugh with them now.

Flo   'My heart is swelling.'

Bel   That's exactly what she was like! (*To* **Annie**.) She's got you perfect.

Flo   And I know it's not the only thing that was swelling either.

Bel laughs.

Annie (*half-playing*)   Flo! –

Flo   What! –

Annie   – Juvenile. –

Flo   – What, your *fiancée* doesn't turn you on?

Annie   – Why do you have to always – it was a nice moment /

Flo   Deny it though! Deny it! Deny it!

Annie   – and you have to take it and make it . . . (*To* **Bel**.) Don't listen to this bitch.

Flo *lets out a dramatic gasp.*

Flo (*still playing*)   Fanny Annie how dare you!

Annie'*s face drops – this is unwelcome teasing.*

Bel *giggles before registering* **Annie**'*s reaction.*

Silence.

Flo (*making light*)   That's it, that's the line, we just found the line.

Small beat.

Flo   You did call me a bitch.

Annie *counts quietly to herself, breathing deeply.*

Flo (*to* **Bel**)   It was a joke that stuck. I shouldn't have said it. Mine was BTS but I worked very fucking hard to unstick that one.

Bel   BTS?

Flo   Big Tits Simmons and before you say anything no they weren't, I was just the first in our year to get them.

Bel   Yeah Flo is better.

Flo   Much better. More me.

B SINGING TO HERSELF

Bel   This is unbelievable. Look at us! What time even is it?

Annie   Yep, that's what happens.

Bel   I like Flo.

Annie   I know you do.

Bel   She's a lot of fun.

Annie   She is that, yeah.

Bel   You're different around her.

Annie   Everyone is.

Bel   You had fun.

Annie   Yeah. I did. I always have fun, she's fun.

Bel   I'm sensing a . . . a thing. This is a thing.

Annie   It's not a thing.

Bel   Yes it is.

Annie   No it's just, I know her better than you, and she's not all that all the time. And, in a way she is and that's exhausting.

Bel   Do you not like her?

Annie   I like her. She's my oldest friend. There's no thing.

Bel   Did you two have a thing?

Annie   No. No, we did not. I've just grown up and she hasn't.

Bel   Have I not grown up either?

Annie   I didn't say that. That's not what I said is it. I'm glad you like her, I'm glad you had fun with her, and she's a good friend, she's an old friend, and this isn't a, it's just we'll see her a lot. That's what she does. She sort of, takes over.

Bel   Like that ant fungus.

Annie   What?

Bel   That zombie ant fungus on the programme.

Annie   No? What?

Bel   Maybe you were working late. The fungus that invades ants and changes their brain and makes them climb to the top of a tree and when they get there the fungus grows because it's near the light. The ant body is just a puppet now; really, it's the fungus.

Annie Well, not that dramatic, but, but she does have a habit of, just . . . I mean, she's good fun and that's it. You think you scratch the surface and you get a deeper, but there is no deeper. There's nothing else – she's all icing and no cake. And she doesn't know – I think she genuinely – I think she's basically psychopathic. She genuinely doesn't know when she is pissing people off. That she is pissing people off, you know tonight even tonight when she whirling dervishes herself around, calling me that when she knows I hate it.

Bel But she apologised for that.

Annie Yeah she apologises all the time, she doesn't change.

Bel And the drink was genuinely an accident.

Annie Sorry, why do you care so much?

Bel I care about you! And I had a really nice time with your really nice friend and I don't quite get why you don't like her if you've been friends such a long time.

Annie I do like her! I really like her! I just think, I just think (*frustrated sigh*) it's good she lives wherever the fuck she lives because when we see each other we have a really good time and then she leaves and that's actually perfect. Because you know, she's this, bundle of energy all the time. She's like a puppy.

Bel So you're mad at a puppy?

Annie Yeah no I know that it's innocent, but why does she get to be the puppy? Why does she get to wag her tail and piss all over everything and I always have to be the human being who cleans it up? Why does she get to be the puppy! Why does no one expect her to be the human being! And why can't I be the puppy!

Bel I'd like to see puppy you.

Small beat.

Annie I'm just really tired. I'm not used to being . . .

> **Bel** *goes to* **Annie** *and pulls her earrings off of her*
> *ears tenderly, placing them in* **Annie**'s *hand.* **Annie**
> *calms down as this happens, then rubs her lobes.*

Bel   They look so sore.

Annie   They're fine.

> **Bel** *kisses* **Annie**'s *ears, then they*
> *gently press their foreheads together.*

Bel   Is it that she's staying this time? Is that stressing
you out?

Annie   She's not staying. She always says that.

A SWELL OF SONG
F BREATHES RHYTHMICALLY, AS IF RUNNING

> **F** *has been exercising, perhaps running,*
> *perhaps on the beach, only a little out of breath.*

A   You don't have an answerphone.

F   No.

A   I've been calling.

F   We don't have an answerphone.

A   I'm glad you're still . . . [together]

F   What are you doing here? Why are you here?

A   Looking for you. Well, for . . . You look . . .

F   I look?

A   Different.

F   Well, it's been, hasn't it.

A   This luck. I just got here and here you . . . [are] I've got
a / room in a tiny B and B . . .

F So what you, what you, just show up?

A I just / remembered . . .

F What do you want?

A Yes, so, the reason I've been trying to get in touch with you – both, actually . . . I've been doing a lot of work on myself. And I just need to say some things to some people and I would like to say sorry. To both of you. But Bel especially, obviously. For the way I . . . reacted. Behaved. It was, the situation was, I should not have done that. Um. I guess I've already, this is me already doing it but I want to do it properly so if there was a good time? For that?

F There's not really a, good time. Bel is . . . Bel doesn't want to see you.

A She knows I'm here?

F No, obviously.

A She doesn't know I'm here.

F She's not going to want to see you.

Beat.

A Ok yeah, ok, yep. Fine. Can I . . . call? Is there a time when you'll pick up?

F I don't think that's a great idea either. No.

A What if I wrote it down. Would you give it to her.

No response from **F**.

A Sorry, this isn't . . . This is not how I planned to . . . I wanted to do it properly. Because you're right because . . . Is there a good time? Please? When we can just, you know sitting down or something? Or now? Are you hungry?

F Maybe another time.

A Ok. Good. I'll call you again, so we can set a time. Yeah?

Beat.

A   I'm here to put things right.

Beat.

F   How long are you going to be here for?

A   I didn't know how long it would take, because I couldn't get through. I didn't know if you were even . . .

F   How did you know we'd be here?

A   I remembered the . . . her house. The place. And then I looked and she was listed.

F   We're listed?

A   If you have a landline, yeah.

Beat.

F (*getting out her phone*)   Give me your number.

> **F** *gives* **A** *her phone – it's a very old model.*

> **A** *plugs in her number.*

A (*giving her the phone back*)   That takes me back.

F   I'll call you. We'll sort a time.

A   Bel doesn't –

F   Don't come – and don't call the house. It's disturbing, alright? She gets disturbed.

A   Alright, yeah, sorry.

F   No it's ok.

A   No I'm sorry.

F   No it's fine, but just, stop doing it. And don't come to the house. I'll call.

B SINGING

*F watches **B** for a moment.*

F   You've been in the garden.

B   I planted all the geraniums.

F   All of them?

B   And cleared out the . . . the . . . the . . . oh the . . .

F   The hut?

B   Yes.

F   All on your own?

B   Yes I / have.

F   I wish / you wouldn't do that.

B   Stop it stop it / stop it.

F   No come / on.

B   Flo Flo please.

F   The thought of you – because / what if . . .

B   Quiet! Shh! Look!

F does.

B   Aren't they great.

F   Ok. They are great.

B   And I didn't die.

F   And you didn't die.

B   In fact I would class this as a triumph, wouldn't you.

F   I suppose so, yes, actually.

B   I did it all. No help necessary.

F   Actually yeah well done.

B   Thank you.

F   Do you feel different?

B   No. Just achey.

The smallest of pauses.

B   What about you?

F   Mm?

B   How was town?

F   Fine.

B   Any adventures?

F   None.

Small beat.

F   Coffee?

B   What time is it?

F   Well, I'm having some.

B   That's a mistake and you know it, Flo.

Music playing.

Bel bops along while Flo physically drags Annie to dance.

Annie   / It's not that I don't want – I'm really exhausted – I – I have been –

Flo   Come on you'll feel better, you'll see, it'll energise you it's the opposite, believe me – come on I just want you to have fun, / have fun with us, look we're having fun, just let your hair down – come on, for me, for me, just one – look at Bel! –

Annie   I am having fun, I am having fun, I am having –
people have fun in different ways – my hair is down, my hair
is literally down.

Flo   – Isn't Bel sexy. Doesn't your sexy fiancée make you
want to move your body. Doesn't she.

Annie   That is not fair. How can I disagree with that.

Flo   Exactly the point. (*Half to* **Bel**.) I know what I'm doing.

> **Bel** *is encouraging* **Annie** *to dance.*

> **Annie** *submits and dances up to* **Bel**.

Flo   Yes! Yes yes yes yes yes! This has to be your wedding
dance song! Wouldn't that be amazing!

> **Flo** *sings along with the song.*

Flo   Sing! Sing!

Annie   I can't / sing . . .

Bel   You can!

Flo   Sing anyway!

Bel   Everyone can sing.

Flo (*to* **Bel**)   You can sing though, I've heard you are a
singer! You sing!

Bel   Oh no, everyone's going to . . .

Flo   What everyone? It's dead, it's a crypt. It needs your
voice!

> *After a beat of reluctance,* **Bel** *sings.*

Flo   Beautiful! Beautiful! God you're beautiful, we're all so
beautiful, look at us. And you know what who cares if it's Not
Official. What, you need some het in a dress to make it
legitimate? Some piece of paper at the end? It's the
ceremony, the symbol, the statement. 'We're getting married
whether you let us or not!' I say go all out. Go all fucking
out, the cake the flowers all of it.

Annie   What have you had?

Flo   Nothing I'm just high on, just fucking life! And love! And life! Look at how alive we are! We are perfection! I'm just high on – but I do have some, some something, something . . .

> **Flo** *pats herself down, looking for whatever drug it is she has.*

> **Bel** *and* **Annie** *are now dancing holding hands or arms.*

Flo   I had something . . . Wait I'll get it.

> *She exits and* **Annie** *relaxes, almost slumps into* **Bel**, *her arms wrapped around her shoulders for support.*

Bel   Are you having a good time?

Annie   Yes.

Bel   Are you sure?

Annie   Yes.

> *They kiss.*

> *Though the song is fast they sink into a slow dance, more a rocking embrace than a dance.*

Flo (*re-entering*)   I need your keys, they might be in the car.

> **Flo** *sees them.*

> *Neither* **Bel** *nor* **Annie** *look back at her.*

> *After a brief moment* **Flo** *rushes to* **Annie**'s *back, throwing her arms around both of them, making it a group hug.*

> **Annie** *rolls her eyes but accepts this – it's actually quite nice.*

> **Bel** *accepts it, but there is a secret beat between her and* **Flo** *when* **Flo**'s *hands fall naturally onto* **Bel**'s *hips.*

> **Flo** *and* **Bel** *hold each other's gaze while* **Annie**'s *eyes are closed.*

> *They rock together.*

BEL – *PANIC ATTACK BREATHING*

Bel *is trying to drink from a large glass of water.*

Flo *is watching from a distance.*

Bel   I have to take it off I can't breathe I can't breathe I can't I'm underwater / I can't breathe I can't I don't know why my lungs they're collapsing I can't breathe . . .

Annie   You can breathe you can breathe shhh breathe in deep stop stop talking stop talking you're alright you're alright it's just me it's just us you're fine I'm with you, I'm with you, I'm here with you – that's better good –

She breathes deeply, leading **Bel***, holding her hands, not once breaking eye contact, her face focused but relaxed.*

Annie   – there – again – . . . – good – you're breathing, you're breathing – bend your knees – you warm?

Bel *nods.*

Annie *has already taken the glass of water, is dipping her fingers into it and smearing it on* **Bel***'s arms, all while they breathe deeply in and out together.*

Annie   There – there . . .

They breathe together like this for a very long time.

Bel *relaxes, swallows.*

Eventually:

Bel   I'll hug you in a minute but it's too tight now.

Annie *nods, understanding.*

They breathe together.

MEDITATION BREATH

Flo *and* **Annie** *are watching* **Bel**,
who is asleep, her head is on **Annie**'s *lap.*

Flo   I'd give anything to sleep like that.

Annie   And me.

Flo   That peace.

Annie   She's got me on this no sugar thing.

Flo   What, none?

Annie   It has actually helped a lot.

Flo   A miracle. She's found a way to make you even more boring.

Annie (*laughing*)   I wasn't boring tonight was I!

Flo   No to be fair you were brilliant tonight.

Annie   I needed tonight.

Flo   So you admit it!

Annie   Work is just stress stress stress.

Flo   Yeah but you love it.

Annie   Less and less. / Poet.

Flo (*in unison with* **Annie**)   Poet.

Annie   I'm tired, way more than tired than – but now I'm in this position where I have to decide all this, everything about every employee and everyone's . . . and it sucks, but someone has to be the bad guy in order for everyone else to be happy. And somehow that bad guy always has to be me.

Flo   Ok but it's alright when you let loose a little isn't it, the world / doesn't end.

Annie Yeah yeah, yes. She did too, I've not seen her like that, especially out. It's nice.

Flo It's the Flo magic.

Beat.

She's great, well done.

Annie She is yeah.

Flo Not your type at all.

Annie She is fit though isn't she.

Flo She is yeah.

Annie It is kind of weird being someone's first.

Flo (*humorously bragging*) You get used to it.

Annie Not first, fully first, but first *full* . . . if that makes sense.

Flo You almost never make sense.

Annie Like she was with girls but it was always . . .

Flo Illicit.

Annie Secret, yeah. Only kissing.

Flo I hate that. Properly hate that. Hiding who you are.

Annie Ooh political.

Flo Not by choice.

Annie Are you still shagging your way across the world then or is there someone, a particular person anywhere?

Flo It's like you don't know me at all.

Annie What you wouldn't like it?

Flo Yeah I would but I'm not looking for it, I'm going to let it come to me.

Annie   It would be nice to see you with someone though. Long term.

Flo   Six months is long term is it?

Annie   Well, at this age . . .

Flo   'This age'! Listen to yourself, you're only twenty-six!

Annie   Twenty-seven.

Flo   I'm twenty-nine! Chill out. We'll get much older than this eventually. What did your mum say?

Annie   Oh don't, she's already booked us dress appointments, she's gone full-on.

Flo (*laughing*)   Fuck that. I mean I can't exactly see you up on the platform with those bulldog clips down your back.

Annie   But I feel like I should because she's accepted her, which was hard won.

Flo   I know.

Annie   Right, you know.

Flo   What are her folks like?

Annie   I don't know because I haven't met them.

Flo   When's that going to happen?

Annie   Never.

Flo   Never?

Annie   Yeah so –

>   *She checks* **Bel** *is definitely asleep.*

Annie   – . . . She hasn't seen them in a decade.

Flo   What! No!

Annie   Yes. They – it's fucked up.

Flo   What they, because / she's –?

Annie (*nodding dramatically*)   All of that.

Flo   Oh my God.

Annie   Yeah.

Flo   So this is illicit too.

Annie   No. Or, not intentionally. If they had any contact, she would. I think she would.

Flo   They big-time religious?

Annie   She doesn't really like to talk about it but I'm guessing so. / –

Flo   Annie, you're marrying this woman and you don't –?

Annie   – From what she's said. What she did tell me was that someone saw her kissing another girl and told them and that was it. Immediately. She was fifteen, she moved out.

Flo   Big family?

Annie   No, just one sister but this is the other crazy thing – that sister, you ready for this? That sister keeps sending her money, it'll just show up in her account. But – *but* – they haven't spoken in ten years either.

Flo   What.

Annie   Yeah. So it's like proper guilt money.

Flo   Has she tried to talk to them.

Annie   Won't.

Flo   Not even / to let them know?

Annie   It got, with her parents, it got physical. / I don't know how bad –

Flo   Oh fucking Christ.

Annie   – had to drag that much out of her, but it got, I think, yeah.

Flo   Poor fucking petal.

Annie   Right at the start I would kiss her and I'd hold her face and she'd . . . (*Gestures 'no'.*) It was really sad. So no I've not met any of them. No, I lie, I've met her, an aunt I think. She lives in Manchester. Or she did, she died. We didn't go to the funeral.

A shared beat.

Annie   So I don't know if the panic attacks are just general anxiety or . . . And she's studying and she's enjoying that and I'm glad she's doing it but it's all from home and she's got nothing to leave the house for, so / she . . .

Flo   How much money does she get from this sister?

Annie   Well, we're buying a house with it. / –

Flo   Yeah she said, so loads then.

Annie   – Well, she is.

Flo   I'll be honest, it sounds like a dump.

Annie (*laughing*)   It is.

Flo   And out in the middle of nowhere? How do you say that place again?

Annie   I don't know I don't know, fucking Welsh.

Flo   Fucking beautiful Welsh.

Annie   But, (*shrugging*) it's what she wants. It's her money.

Flo   And you? Is it what you want?

Beat.

Annie   I want her.

SURFING BREATH – DEEP, FROM
THE DIAPHRAGM, STRONG
THEN HELD
THEN RELEASED

Flo   I'll do anything to keep surfing. The crazy shit I've
done to keep doing that – I've worked bars and taught
gymnastics and dressed up like a cat for an office party, an
office leaving party. I don't care, I'll do it. Before surfing, my
life, fuck my life was a disaster. Waking up every morning
and having nothing, nothing to wake up for. I'd never had
anything I cared about and it was sort of normal but I still
felt – I knew it wasn't normal. To feel that way. All the time.
So it's not a joke when I say surfing changed my life – people
say this shit about horses or whatever it is, it saves their lives
and it sounds like bunk but it's true, because everything is in
service of that now – I have jobs to earn money to keep
surfing. I have to take care of my health, my body, to keep
surfing. I have friends now. I didn't really have friends
before, apart from Annie, and that was just proximity, you
know? Just growing up near each other, just both being gay,
you know, doesn't mean you share anything else together.
She was always . . . We were just really different, but good
mates but you know, different. It's amazing what that
woman can do. It's cool. She used to fly off the handle a lot
when we were growing up, because she had a lot of trouble
with like, who she was, who she – I'm sure you know all
about it. And I mean a lot, it was scary, and then one day
after a particularly bad thing she says to me 'I'm going to
stop doing that' and she does. She just does. Starts
exercising, running, instead. It was weird and creepy even
but it's discipline. And I didn't understand that. Until
surfing. Honestly it, it changed my life. It's like the army, but
for hippies. It takes me all over the world and I can go
anywhere in the world where there's a swell – you need a
storm to get one – and I'll see someone I know. Like how
amazing is that. I'm free to do – and I'm free in the water, it

sounds like a cliché but it really really is, it's like those flying dreams. Not flying, because I've done that, been up in the air, but flying in your dreams, it's different. It's really . . . you should try it.

Bel   That's how I felt in choir. The same . . . what did you call it?

Flo   Call what?

Bel   The thing that makes the wave.

Flo   Swell.

Bel   Right. That's it. In your chest, but also in your heart, you feel that. Sounds so stupid out loud.

Flo   Not stupid. Not stupid. You don't do it any more?

Bel   No. Can't. Don't like the, environment.

Flo   All the people?

Bel   Yeah basically. Which I hate because that's what I used to love about it, being part of something so much bigger than, being a small part of something big. Losing yourself in that. But when, when I, when, when everyone found out, about me, suddenly I wasn't the person – I wasn't part of them, couldn't be part of, it. But I loved, disappearing. Into other people. Dissolving in vibrations. Is that what it feels like? When you, is it called wipe out?

Flo (*joke-bragging*)   I almost never wipe out. But yeah.

Beat.

Bel   It must be terrifying. Out there on your own, water all around you.

Flo   I'm never alone. You never surf alone, unless you're a nutcase – for the record I am just the right side of nutcase. No there's always people watching out for you, there's a community, no matter if you've known them for twenty seconds or twenty years, that's what's brilliant about it, it doesn't matter, it's the same. I couldn't do it if it weren't for that, that community. (*Humour.*) I'm not very good at being alone.

Bel   I think you are. I think we both are.

Flo *is a little uncomfortable for the first time.*

Bel   What particularly bad thing?

Flo   I don't even remember now. Some thing with a girl. There's a gay choir in Plymouth, sort of near me, they're supposed to be really good. I've never actually been. Too, regular, commitment. You could, that would be a new way to – and I'm sure there's one near here, they're all over.

Bel   Really?

Flo   Oh yeah they're everywhere, very big in the scene.

Bel   I don't know anything about the scene, I feel really stupid.

Flo   Alright, well, I'm taking you out on the scene, I'm educating you. You need to meet the other special people. There are so many of us. You'll fall in love every day.

Bel   I'd like that.

A SWELL OF SONG

Just before dawn.

F   People will think we've committed some sort of crime.

B   We're old. It's normal to be up this early when you're old.

F   Let's stroll at least.

B   It's coming – the sky, look.

F   Move our bodies. Get some distance from the drunk teens and the people walking their aggressive dogs.

B   Two drunk teens, one reactive dog.

F   And we're not that old.

B   Why can't you just pause and / take this in.

F   Though I do catch myself in the mirror, stepping out of the shower, and my blood pressure spikes: 'Who the fuck is that?'

B   This is why I wanted to do this. You're jumpy lately.

F   I'm not 'jumpy'.

B   There's a study, it's my favourite study – ok, my latest favourite study – they talked to all these different people of all these different ages, every age, and they asked them two questions. The first was, 'How much have you changed in the last five years?' And everyone said, 'Oh, I've changed so much in the last five years.' And then their second question was, 'How much do you think you will change in the next five years?' And everyone, everyone said, 'Not that much.'

They both find the irony funny.

F   God, no, no more change. I've done enough changing.

B   Do you feel, um, feel . . .

F   Yeah?

B   Uh . . .

F   Is it negative or positive?

B   Huh?

F   The word you're looking for.

B   I'm not looking, I'm . . . hesitating. Because, I do feel, um . . . guilty.

F   Guilty?

B   For changing your – well, your whole life.

F   That's not / . . .

B It wasn't just me, my life, that changed.

F For the better. For the better, for me. Even with all the
. . . And doing the town stuff for you, for us, it's a small
price. (*Reassuring, lightening.*) Look what I get for it.

B Ok.

Beat.

B Um. You unplugged the phone.

F . . . I didn't think you'd notice, honestly. Sorry.

B Why did you unplug the phone?

F I . . . (*breath*) . . . Bel . . . I've lied to you.

F and B have stopped walking.

B . . . Ok. I did think, something . . . Ok. Ok. Tell me.

F I . . . I'm sorry. I . . .

F and B are looking at each other.

They are both readying themselves.

F . . . didn't uh pay it. Forgot.

B (*relief*) Oh.

F We really have to modernise. (*Walking again.*) Direct
debit, that sort of thing. We're almost Amish at this point,
someone's going to be round any minute to make a
documentary –

B is craning her neck up and back,
trying not to cry – she looks odd.

F – they'd think we were – oh oh oh oh no, no no, / oh no,
no –

B What – what? What?

F Are you having –?

B No no, no I'm just / –

F   Sit down.

B   I'm just trying not to – my eyes / . . .

F (*physically moving her*)   Lie down.

B   No I'm not – stop! Stop! I just had tears, I just wanted not to – I was welling up, I was trying not to cry.

F   What's the matter?

B   Nothing's the matter!

F   Why are you crying!

B   Stop being like this! I'm fine!

F   That's easy for you, for you to say! Just say! Isn't it! But I have to be on the lookout, all / the time, it's easier for you!

B   You can't keep thinking / like that . . .

F   You could have been having another stroke!

B   It's been years!

F   Yes, and everyone said you'd be dead years ago.

B   And I'm *not*.

F   It doesn't mean – it means you're *more* likely to have another.

B   I hate seeing you like this. And I know there's nothing I can do. Because I'm me, because of me. And I just think maybe, I think you are holding everything, on your own, for me, and you've done that for such a long time – for years. But maybe, now . . .

F   We're not breaking up *now*.

B (*laughing – a release*)   No.

They laugh together.

B   But you need someone else, some support. Some friends. You're always moaning that your parents are always moaning that they don't see you enough . . .

F   I see them enough.

B   Maybe you should see them more than once a year.

F   I like things the way things are. Is it that you want, more? Is that what you're really saying?

B   I have what I want. I don't want more.

They walk again.

B   I like it this early. This late. Them being the same thing, it's calming. That sky.

Beat.

B   Did we do the right thing?

Long pause.

B   Do you think we did the right thing?

F   Not right for everybody. But. Right for us.

Bel   I just think it would be fun, it would be exciting.

Annie   We'd lose all the money.

Bel   We'd lose the money we've paid but we'd save money, the money that we're *going* to pay on everything.

Annie   Yeah but we've made deposits.

Bel   Yeah but I'm not talking about the mathematics. I'm talking about you and me in love and that's it. We could just fuck off, we could do it anywhere, (*joking*) we could go to Vegas!

Annie   We can't get married in Vegas –

Bel   We can have a a a . . .

Annie You want / to go to Vegas?

Bel I want to marry you. I don't want to marry all those other people so why do they have to be there?

Annie But you are, you know with me you / get my mother and . . .

Bel I know I get that I'm just saying, I just don't want to wait. I'm just finding everything . . . And what if we just said screw it and left and did it on our own somewhere beautiful, not Vegas, somewhere amazing. Just us.

Annie Look, I know what this is.

Bel What?

Annie I know why you're doing this.

Beat.

Bel What do you mean?

Annie Bel, I know what's going on.

Silence.

Bel You know?

Annie Of course I do. It's obvious. And I get it. I know it's hard for you, I know you're scared, I know you're anxious about the crowd, but believe me, when you've done it, when you've looked out at everyone and done this with me you'll feel so much better. I did. It was the best thing I ever did. Not immediately, but eventually. I used to be so angry at everything and it changed me. You don't have to hide anymore, Bel. You can be who you are, you don't have to hide with me. We're not hidden. You don't have to keep doing that now. This is your new life, saying to everyone – this is me, this is the woman I love.

Bel *is very agitated.*

Annie I'll be there. With you. By your side. We can have a safety word. Any time you feel panicky or anxious it'll / be a code word.

Bel I don't need a code word it's not about a code word it's about all of it, all of it. It's about the family and the friends and you and . . . and . . .

Annie Me?

Bel The the the wedding . . .

Annie Bel, I don't know what you're talking about, I don't know what . . .?

Bel Ok, so, ok . . . ok . . . I . . . I'm so . . .

Annie Come on spit it out, you're pissing me off now.

Bel can't.

Annie What are you trying to say? What, you don't love me?

Bel I do love you.

Annie Then what – then what . . . have you – has something . . . is it something I – what have I done?

Bel No it's not no it's nothing you've it's – it's . . . It's someone else.

Beat.

Annie Someone else?

Beat.

Annie Who. Who!

She starts counting but doesn't get all the way to ten.

Bel I really didn't think, intend, for . . . for . . . I'm / so sorry.

Annie Have you been, what – what?

Bel I didn't want – have any intention / for this –

Annie   What do you mean intention. This is – this has – has it? Has something? Is this / just, or . . .

Bel   We never thought / . . .

Annie   'We'! We!

Bel   But it wasn't, I meant to say something / but I . . .

Annie   Who's we! Who's we! Who's we!

Bel   Flo.

Beat.

Annie   Flo?

> **Annie** *is quieter now, more still, but far from calm.*

Bel   She's . . . She just, she just makes sense. More sense.

Annie   No you don't make sense you make no sense – you can't leave the house / –

Bel   Don't make that – don't . . .

Annie   – and she can't sit still for two seconds, you're not making sense. You're – you're just, new, and excited, and greedy.

Bel   I'm not good at all this stuff, this family stuff and / office parties . . .

Annie (*breathing, struggling*)   I can – you don't have to – I'll spend more time at home. I know I can be, with the job, but I can pull back / I can . . .

Bel   No that's your, you need to do that.

Annie   I'll do whatever! Whatever it is I'll – we don't have to get married at all if that's that's really what you / want we don't have to.

Bel   That's not, that's not . . .

Annie   Well, what is it! What is it then! What is it about me! About her and not me why not me!

Beat.

Annie   Because I know, I know, Bel, that you love me. I know you do. It's something I know, know past knowing, you love me. Stand there and tell me you don't love me.

Bel   I do love you.

Annie   Don't reassure me, tell me. Tell me you don't love me. Say you don't love me.

Bel *can't.*

Annie   You know I love you don't you?

Bel *nods.*

Annie   Know past knowing.

Bel *nods.*

Annie   So why are you doing this? Are you actually doing this? What, I don't make you happy? I have done – given you – and I'll do anything . . .

Bel   I'm / sorry.

Annie   Three months ago you wanted to marry / me and now you . . .

Bel   *You* wanted to get married! You and your mother was so keen to fucking shove us down the aisle.

Annie   Nobody forced you!

Bel   But there was so much pressure!

Annie   Why are you telling me now! Why didn't you – why did you have to fuck my friend to figure out / you didn't want . . .

Bel   You don't make it easy to / talk to you.

Annie   Oh no no I'm not having you blaming me for this. Was it her? Was it her coming on to you? She does that, she does that with everyone. Do you love her?

Beat.

Annie   Do you love her? Do you love her?

Small beat.

Annie   Do you love her? –

> **Bel** *goes to* **Annie** *as she asks this but*
> *when she touches her* **Annie** *lashes out.*

Annie   Do you love her! Do you! Do you!

Bel *tries to free herself but in response* **Annie** *tightens her grip.*

Annie   You do don't you!

With this **Annie** *throws* **Bel** *against something, or to the ground.*

They both immediately halt.

Bel *is hurt.*

Annie   Are you ok?

Bel *is silent.*

Annie   Are you ok?

Bel   I'm fine.

Annie   I'm sorry.

Bel *can't respond.*

Annie   Are you ok?

Bel   Yes I'm fine.

Annie   No let me look, / you're – are you hurt?

Bel   No no I'm alright it'll be fine.

Annie   I'll get you some ice.

Bel   No don't I don't / need – ice.

> **Annie** *has already gone.*
>
> **Bel** *rubs the place of contact.*

B SINGING
THE OTHERS JOIN
A SWELL OF SONG
B REPEATING HERSELF STRANGELY –
THE RYTHMN FRAYS, DISINTEGRATES

Silence.

Annie   A clot. There was some swelling, from the, the
contusion. But, it was a clot. Of blood. That . . . it got stuck. In
the – they say, they said, like a marble in a hose pipe, and
there are all these different sized hose pipes in the brain and
this marble fit this hosepipe perfectly. And got just lodged
there. And stayed. In the, FFA, the something facial area. It's
the part of the brain, it's the bit of the brain that has a lot to do
with a lot of stuff, so they don't know what's going to be
affected, if anything, hopefully not anything, but they've
talked about, you know, amnesia, not remembering,
memories . . . Not being able to speak. And not being able to
use bits of her body like one side. She does look different but
I can't tell if that's me thinking she's going to look different so
seeing it, seeing her different. She looks like, herself but not
herself. But . . . maybe it's just because she's, lying that way.
So. We're still finding out how bad, what damage exactly.

Flo   A clot?

Annie   A clot, yeah.

Flo   But she's so, but that's . . . an old person thing. She's
young.

Annie   Apparently it can happen to anyone.

Flo   Just randomly like that?

Annie   Just randomly.

Flo   Why would she have a clot she / was so healthy.

Annie   I don't know they say it's from anything. It can be from anything, a cut or a bruise or a, a, a scrape / or –

Flo   What's a contusion?

Annie   She has a – she cut her, knocked her, head.

Flo   How?

Annie   But they say anything, anything, any kind of injury. From years ago even.

Flo   Years ago?

Annie   Not years / ago . . .

Flo   Because it would dissolve? Right?

Annie   I don't know.

Flo   You don't think . . . You don't think / –

Annie   I don't know!

Beat.

Annie   It's possible.

Beat.

Annie   So. That's what's happening.

Flo   She's awake?

Annie   Not right now.

Flo   She's sleeping now?

Annie   I'm not waking her up.

Flo   No don't wake her I'm not asking to wake her don't wake her, I'm just checking. She's not unconscious she's just asleep?

Annie   Yeah she's just sleeping. She was unconscious for . . . But now she's asleep.

Flo   She's been awake?

Annie   I wasn't there but yes, she'll wake up again and, and you can . . . talk. I'll leave / you to . . .

Flo   No I, I. No you can – I can leave you to . . .

Annie   Look, I'm / not going to . . .

Flo   I, look . . . Ok, this is, obviously this is so much. I did not, I'm sorry I . . . I can't be – you know she's going to need a carer. She's going to need . . .

Annie   There might be nothing.

Flo   No Annie, no, I've seen it. Strokes . . . There's this guy in Newquay . . . He can't even . . . She's going to . . . I didn't, I can't, this is, this isn't, this kind of – I can't.

Beat.

Flo   Fuck! . . . I can't do this. I can't. I'm sorry. I'm sorry for so much, and I'm sorry for this too because I can't I can't talk to I can't I've got to go. I'm going to go. And look tell her . . .

Beat.

Flo   Yeah just tell her I'm sorry. Just tell her I'm so sorry that I couldn't, that I wasn't, that I was tell her I was . . . That's not who I . . . Please. Please do that. I know you don't have to you don't have to do anything you shouldn't do anything for me, but if you could do that.

Beat.

Annie   Don't worry. Go ahead. I'll tell her exactly what you decided to do. Do you think she'll be surprised?

Flo *stares back at* **Annie**.

F   It's wildly specific. The brain is so complex that basically anything can happen. So there's this guy, who's kept everything except he's lost verbs. So he can speak normally, he has normal conversations, but he can't access any verbs. There's someone who can only say 'tono', it might be his name I'm not sure. And then there's people who lose the ability to speak at all, speech loss of some sort is the most common outcome but Bel can speak completely fine.

A   Really.

F   Yep, completely.

A   Fantastic.

F   Yep.

A   So what is it with her then?

F   So she has a few things, what she has, it's amazing really, the brain – so one thing is that the signals come in from her eyes or her ears or whatever it is but the brain ignores half of it. So if she's looking at the clock she'll see 12-1-2-3-4-5-6, and she won't see 7-8-9-10-11.

A   What, her vision?

F   No, her vision works fine, and the connections are all there, but when the whole clock goes up to the brain, the brain responds by saying 'fuck 7 to 11'.

A   No.

F   Yeah. And when we have dinner she eats half of her plate / –

A   No.

F   – and then I just spin it round and she eats the other half. And then dressing, she can dress herself, she has good mobility, sometimes she has trouble with her left side but that's mostly because she just forgets about her left side, so she's always forgetting her socks and her shoes on that side. She doesn't comb that side of her hair. So it's mostly just about reminding her.

A   What about her memory?

F   Memory's intact.

A   What completely?

F   Absolutely.

A   That's fantastic.

F   Yeah. The main thing is, this is the main thing – she can't attach things in her head. It's not memory, it's – in the hospital she remembered everything, everyone, but she'd mix up – she kept thinking her big, huge, male nurse was her sister. She knew who her sister was, she knew where she was, and why, she wasn't confused, she just kept thinking it was her sister walking through that door. And so now, so she can ask for a knife, and I can give her a knife, and she can hold the knife in her hand, but she won't know what it is. She'll know what a knife is, and she'll be able to see the thing in her hand, what it feels like and everything else, all it's other defining . . . and she can't connect it. Until I tell her. So I'm, constantly making those connections for her, telling her what things are.

A   Still?

F   The brain does repair itself, makes new pathways, she's come on so far, but those things have persisted.

A   That's so sad.

F   It's not sad. It's just something to work around. To work with. She has strategies, lists in her head. You know they say 'good days and bad days', that's really true. And she, and it can be stressful. But. She stays in the house, she likes it there, the house is small but the land is big and she potters around. She does a lot of yoga, which has really helped, forces her to use that left side of her or she falls over. You know, she's never been good with crowds, but even coming into this little town is too – she has this – well, anyway, it's stressful. So she just stays in and I do the shopping and all the other stuff. It's a pretty simple life. And um, we're just really happy.

A (*pleased*)   Really.

F   Yes really.

A   No I'm not I'm – I'm really happy you're still together.

F   You thought we wouldn't be.

A   I didn't know. After all that . . . I'm so glad you stayed.

F   Well, it was the right thing to do. I wanted to.

A   Can I . . .

Beat.

A   What I did was inexcusable. You loved each other. I should never have, got in the way of that. Whatever my own . . . And I should definitely / not have . . .

F   Love. Present tense.

A   Of course.

Pause.

A   I was thinking, I could, help?

F   What do / you mean help?

A   I've got a bit of money now, I could come round and see you both and see if . . . And help.

F   You mean give us money?

A   Just like, see if you need anything.

F   Why would we need anything from you?

A   I just wanted to see you both and see how you were and and you're happy and it's fantastic. I'm sorry.

F   What about. For what.

A   For everything.

Beat.

A   I am. I'm not asking for your – I'm not expecting you . . . Do you accept my . . . can you accept . . . can you receive, that I'm sorry?

F   Yeah. Yes. I, I accept it.

A (*moved*)   Thank you.

F   You're welcome.

A   It's been with me this whole time. And I'd really like to do the same with Bel.

F   I really don't think. Really. No.

A   I know that / she needs . . .

F   It's not possible, sorry.

A   Please.

F   It's not fair on her, she's my priority, you aren't / –

A   I know I –

F   – we've moved on.

A   I just want her to / know . . .

F   She still hasn't forgiven you.

Small beat.

F   She doesn't want to. She can't. I'm sorry.

Pause.

Text tone – **F** *takes out her phone.*

F   Her ears must have been burning.

A *doesn't respond.*

F *tries to diffuse the awkwardness:*

F   How are you? I haven't asked that. Tell me how you are, what you've been up to.

A   Nothing. Nothing. The same. Same everything. It's getting . . . anyway.

Pause.

F   Is there, anyone? Any girlfriend?

A   I did have, I did have, but she . . . They just don't, um, stick around. That's happened quite a lot actually.

F   Fuck I'm sorry.

A   No it's alright. Things aren't ever the way you want them are they. It just feels like this is the compromise I'm having to make to . . . Basically I've got my life and that's, that's . . . And basically I'm never what they want. I'm exciting for a second, and then, something else is exciting.

> **F** *reaches out to comfort* **A** *with a touch, sort of without realising she's doing it.*

> **F** *pulls her hand back.*

> **A** *reaches out to take her hand in hers.*

> *After a beat they both exhale, a weird relief.*

A   We should have done this a long time ago.

F   You might be right.

A   How long have we known each other?

F   Well, there's been a gap. But yeah. Most of our lives.

A   Isn't that crazy.

F   It is. Feels like longer.

> *A small shared laugh.*

F   Do you remember meeting?

A   No.

F (*laughing a little*)   Me neither.

A   I thought you were going to say.

F   I thought you would.

They laugh.

A   And you know what . . . Yeah I'm just going to say this, I'm really glad nothing happened between us. I think that was . . . the right thing.

Beat.

F   Ok(?)

A   Yeah. I hope that's ok to say.

F   Why did – it's fine, just, why are you saying it?

A   Well, you know . . .

F   Go on.

A   We've just known each other a long time. There was a lot of time, and you – we never, and I know that must have been hard, that's all.

F   Hard?

A   For you not to . . . to do anything.

F   With you?

A   And you know, I was such a mess, I probably would have done whatever.

F   That is . . . that is . . .

A   What?

F   That is so arrogant.

A   What?

F   You are – you are incredible.

A   Come on.

F   Come on what.

A   I know, I've always known you wanted something. That's / why you –

F   Look this was a bad idea I should never – I'm going to go cancel the order – or pay, / just pay if they won't let me . . .

She rummages for her wallet.

A   No don't, come on we can be honest now, can't we. I'm saying I'm glad nothing happened, because / your friendship . . .

F   Nothing happened because I didn't want it to happen. Not because I couldn't have you because you're right you weren't exactly a challenge to get into bed were you. I didn't sleep with you because I didn't like you. (*Leaving.*) Not everyone wants to fuck you.

She leaves with her wallet.

A *relaxes, sadly.*

She sees that **F** *has left her phone.*

A *looks to where* **F** *has exited.*

A *then picks up the phone and finds what she's looking for –* **B**'s *mobile number – and is extremely happy.*

She considers her action for just a moment before dialling the number and putting it to her ear.

B (*off*)   Hi, Flo, don't worry, I found it.

A   Bel?

B (*off*)   Hello? Yeah?

A   Bel, it's – how did, how did you know it was me?

B (*off*)   It came up on my phone.

A   I'm not calling from my phone.

B (*off*)   Yes you are.

At this point **F** *has re-entered.*

A   Has – I – I want to see you . . .

F *snatches the phone from* **A**, *sees who's on the screen and hangs up.*

A *quakes.*

They stare at each other.

A   She thought you were me.

Silence.

A   Why did she think that?

The phone rings.

F, *torn, eventually decides the best action is to
pick up, but she struggles to say something.*

B (*off*)   Flo? Flo? Can you hear me? We cut off. I'm not
hearing anything . . . Can you hear me?

F (*instinctively moving away from* **A**)   Yeah, hi.

B (*off*)   There you are. Is everything alright? You sound
weird?

F   Everything's fine I just . . . I'm coming back soon.

B (*off*)   Ok, nothing else?

F   Yeah, no, just . . . What was it you wanted me to pick up?

B (*off*)   Lemons. Oh and um, oh um, I can see it I just can't
get the name.

F   Asparagus.

B (*off*)   Asparagus, yes. The small ones.

F   Yeah I'll do that.

B (*off*)   Ok, don't hurry back, I'm fine.

F   Ok, I'll be back soon.

B (*off*)   Take your time. Love you.

F   Love you too.

B hangs up.

F   The stroke, she . . . she . . . the stroke really . . . The stroke mixes things up for her. She sometimes, she . . . the stroke . . .

A   Why is she calling you Flo.

F   It's just something she does. It's just because of the stroke /.

A   No. No. She called you Flo. That wasn't a slip-up, why would she slip up, she hasn't seen me in – you didn't correct her. She thought I was you calling. But it was your phone. So what, so my name . . .

Long beat.

F   It's just . . . She just calls me / Flo . . .

A   What is it some, what some, game, some, fetish?

F   It's not a, no, no . . .

A   Is it . . . God. This is / –

F   It's just, she just calls me that.

A   – This is disgusting. And she likes it? She likes when you pretend to be me?

F   It's not pretend! I'm not pretending!

A   This is sick, you're both sick. / It's like you're wearing my skin.

F   I'm not sick! Neither is she! We're happy, we love each other, she loves me, she just / calls me that . . .

A   Why would she call / you that if it wasn't . . .!

F   Because she thinks –!

She stops herself, but too late.

Pause.

F   Because she thinks . . . because she . . . when she . . .

She can't complete her sentence.

Pause.

A   She thinks . . . Ok.

She understands.

A strange calm.

A   That's why you don't want me at the – don't want me showing up? She thinks you're me.

F *can only shake her head*

A   She does, she thinks you're me. She thinks you're me! That's what you meant, she can't attach things. So she sees you . . . You're letting her – fucking hell. Fuck.

F   Please, stop, just . . .

A   Fuck. Annie. What the fuck. She thinks you're me! You're letting her – you're telling her –! Why are you . . .?

F doesn't know what to do or say,
and is barely containing herself.

A   How long has she – it's been thirty years.

F   Twenty-eight years.

A   Shut up! It's been almost thirty years, what – thirty years?! Has she, for thirty years has she –?

F can't respond, and this answers A's question.

She deflates.

A   Annie. Annie. What are you . . . For how long? For the whole, for –?

F   The whole time.

A   I'm going to be sick. There is so much here that is so fucked up. So wrong, so disgusting, so wrong, so . . . I am seeing her. You are going to let me see her.

F   No you are not.

A (*struggling to stop herself from shouting in a public place*)   You can't keep her! Like an animal! In a cage in a tower! Any more!

Beat.

A   This is insane. How have you kept this – it's insane, Annie. It's over. It is ending now. I am ending it.

F   Yeah and then walk away like you always do, you won't be there to deal with it. What is she going to do? If you do that, she'll . . . You'll destroy everything, her whole – our whole – she's been doing so well, you can't / just –

A   You stole my identity!

F   You stole my fiancée!

A   That is fucking stupid I didn't steal anyone. You can't steal people, she left you. She left and you can't handle it. You take her here, away / from everyone –

F   She took me, this is where she wants to be.

A   – Christ, all this time. How dare you. Punish her like this.

F   That is not – I am caring for her.

A   Fuck.

F   I am taking care of her.

A   You're lying to her!

F   That *is* taking care of her! She wanted to be with you so I made that happen. And you know what you should be fucking grateful, because you're the one who fucked off, left her, *left her*, in that [state] – when she was scared and alone and you just left. Because you were too uncomfortable. Too selfish. And when she was calling out for you, I let her have that. Even though it hurt me. It really hurt me. What do you think it's been like for me? You think this is all some fantasy? Couldn't be farther from it. It's been . . . and there've been times – but I stayed, which is more than you ever did for anyone. I did what I had to do, for both of us. Even when she talked – when I had to blame her, her condition for me not being enough like you, acting like you, fucking like you, different to be around – even when I lied to her. I loved her. I love her. And she loves me.

A   No. Annie. She loves me.

F   She loves the person that has been caring for her for the whole second half of her life and that's me! I've done all of it and what have you done. Nothing. You've lived your life, and you come back now that *you* feel that *you* can. You have no idea what it's been like, you have no clue, you're in / no position . . .

A   You are not going to guilt me! Anymore! I will not be guilted by the person who made her this way in the fucking first place!

Silence from **A**.

A   Who else knows. Does anyone else know?

F   No.

A   Her family?

F   No.

A   Your family?

F   No.

A   They will know. Everyone will know, I'll make sure. I will do that.

F   Please don't. Please don't. Please.

A   Let me see her.

Bel *stirs – her movement is very limited.*

They overlap as they speak to each other:

Bel   Oh. Oh my God. Oh my God oh my God.

Annie   I know it's ok you're ok.

Bel   Oh my God I'm so happy you're here I'm so happy ah so happy, thank you – ah – ah oh, wow that hurts. It hurts, I love you.

Annie   I'm sorry, I'll call a / I'll call someone.

Bel   No don't don't don't go don't call.

Annie   Ok.

Bel   I love you so much.

Annie   I love you too.

Bel   Thank – thank – thank – I didn't know if you'd say it back.

Annie   Of course I – of course.

Bel   I love love you I'm happy oh I love you oh help I love you.

They are embracing by now.

Bel   Thank God you said it thank God you're here, thank God you're here thank God. I love you.

Annie   I love you so much. I love you so much.

Bel   I love you too. I love you too. Please don't go don't leave please don't –

Annie   I'm not going to leave.

Bel   – please don't leave me please can we just stay here together.

Annie   Of course. I'm not leaving. I'm not leaving.

Bel   I love you.

Annie   I love you too.

Bel   I'm so happy to see you. I'm so happy it's you, I thought . . .

Annie   Of course I'm here. Of course I came, of course I'm here.

Bel   I love you. Such a relief, I've been so scared.

Annie   I was too. But you're ok.

Bel   You're here, I'm here, you're here.

Annie   I'm here. You're fine. You're talking, that's amazing.

Bel   We're here. I love you. Who else is here?

Annie   Just me. Just you and me it's just you and me.

Bel   I love that. I love that. Wow. Please let's keep it – please don't let her come in.

Annie   I won't.

Bel   Don't let her come in – is she mad?

Small beat.

Annie   She's not coming in.

Bel   I don't want her here, I feel too bad, I feel too bad already, she'll be so mad at me she was so upset –

Annie *is quiet as she processes this.*

Bel   – it'll be too much, please don't let her come in, please.

Annie   Ok.

Bel   Or her family. Don't let her family in. Don't let anyone in, please promise me you won't let her family – they're too much, please, please can it just be you and me. Just you and me in this room together forever and that's it that's all I want. Just you and me. I'm still so – I feel . . . weird. Weird. Things look different, feel weird. I'm scared and I'm very afraid. Please don't let them in.

Annie   I won't. I won't let them in. It's just you and me.

Bel   I love you so much, Flo.

Beat.

Annie   I love you too, Bel.

F BREATHING, SWALLOWING, SUPPRESSING

B   Hello(?)

A   Hi.

B   A visitor. Sorry, we just don't have people over, ever really. Sorry, have we met? I have this little problem, I'm not wonderful with faces.

A   Um, that's ok, we actually, we . . .

F   Bel, this . . . Ok. I . . .

B   Help me out, the name should do it.

F   This is / –

A   You don't recognise me?

B   Um. Sorry.

Beat.

B   It doesn't mean I don't [know you] – I don't recognise anyone. Anyone. It's not you, it's me.

A *is clearly hurt by this, and takes a moment.*

B   I'm sorry. I'll know you I just can't – from just – It's really honestly nothing / to do with . . .

A   We . . . Well we . . .

B   Oh, choir? Am I embarassing myself?

A   Choir?

B   The choir? Is that where we know each other? Sorry, if I saw you in context, in the hall or that street I'd piece it together. It's not Sarah is it?

A   You go to choir?

B   When I can. Love it.

F   Bel, this is . . .

A (*stopping* **F**)   We haven't met.

B   Oh. Oh?

A   No.

B   We haven't?

Small beat.

B   Phew. Ok then. I just feel so rude all the time, sorry. Not that I have to, because, Flo goes out for me, I stay here, because it's just quite tiring.

A   I can imagine. You're . . . You're . . . Sorry, just, you're so . . . You're nothing like I imagined.

B   What did you imagine?

Beat.

A   Not . . .

B   Can I get you a drink, are you staying?

A   I don't know. Maybe. No. No I'm not. I'm going to, I think I'll just go.

B   No stay. If you want to. I was going to make a quiche. If you wanted some quiche? And Flo makes a very exciting salad. She puts fruit and nuts and, and . . . and . . . (*to* **F**) from cows.

F   Cheese.

B   And cheese and all sorts in there, sort of a mismatch of all the places she's been. Don't you. It's barely a salad.

A   I think I'll go. I just wanted to, just see, the house.

B   Oh yes. It's nice isn't it, all Flo. It was really falling apart when we got it. By the sea though, which we both love. Are you a surfing buddy?

A   Yeah. We . . . You've done a good job of it.

B   Flo's quite the handy man, not that she'd let on. With the internet and some commitment you can transform anything, can't you.

F   Yep.

B   Without her . . . Well, my life would be very different. I'd probably still just be camping in the one room that didn't leak, which was the loo, ironically. It was an obstacle course just to get through the house when we first arrived, the doors were all swollen so you couldn't close them properly and if you did you'd be trapped, had to be very careful you didn't just absentmindedly – (*to* **F**) the number of times you rescued me. You're sure we don't know each other?

A   What? No, I'm sure. I thought we had but I think I've seen pictures, or just heard about you or . . . We don't know each other. (*To* **F**.) Do we? We've not met.

F   No, I don't think so. No you haven't.

B   It's just something about the way you're . . . Something about your hands. I don't know, it's all a mess up here. Anyway thank you for dropping by, if you have to go.

A   I do have to go, yes.

B   The most social stimulation I've had in ages. Sounds pretty sad doesn't it, but it's about as much as I can handle to be honest. Even the singing, I mostly just show up and sing. Blend in to everyone else. Submerge. Like I'm alone. I like it. Are you just passing through?

A   Pretty much.

B   From where?

A   Australia.

B   My God!

A   Yeah.

B   You've come a long way.

A   I have. But yes I'll go, yes sorry to . . . I'll go. (*To* **F**.) Good seeing you again, keep in touch. (*To* **B**.) Lovely to meet you.

B   Lovely to meet you.

A   Good to um, to see . . . Just put a name to a . . . I've heard a lot about you.

B   Well, maybe we'll see each other again.

A   Maybe, yep.

F   I'll see you out / . . .

A   No I can – I can do that. I know how to do that. You stay here, I can leave all by myself. (*Sort of joking.*) I'm expert at it.

Small beat.

A   Bye, Flo.

She exits.

B   She was nice.

F (*hiding her emotions badly*)   Yeah.

B   What's the matter? (*Embracing her.*) Come here, tell me. Come on.

F   Nothing, I just. We don't have . . . Visitors are quite stressful, aren't they.

B   Very stressful. I mean they've always been stressful for me.

F   You did really well.

B   Thank you. It felt different I don't know why.

This sets **F** *off.*

B   It's alright. Come on, there. Do you want to lie down?

F   No. I'll make the salad.

B   She was . . . She was . . .

F (*trying to remain composed*)   Was . . .?

B   What do you think she thought?

Beat.

B   Seeing me?

F   You?

B   Not everyone, understands. When they, I think, see me. Here. They see, someone, not free. They don't, understand. That I'm . . . Like you do. Not everyone would . . . like you do. Did.

F   Are you feeling . . . how are you feeling, Bel?

B   She reminded me of someone.

F   Yeah?

B   Guess.

F   Guess who?

B   Yeah.

F   I don't know, who.

B   You. A bit.

F   Really.

B   A younger you. A sort of different you. When we first met. She was very like you were, the sort of, way she held herself. I remember falling so . . . stupidly, so completely, falling for . . . The way you held yourself.

She is looking directly at **F**.

B   And I often think – I hope this doesn't hurt your feelings, I do often think about how stupid I was, actually. How stupid that was. I was stupid.

B speaks very deliberately, very intently, with clarity.

B   And, how lucky I am, that this, this, worked out in the end. Because if it hadn't worked out . . .

She is sending a message between her words.

B   I'd like to apologise to Anais. I should do that, somehow. I should have so long ago. I really was in love with, Anais. On this, deep . . . And, and I really didn't know what to do with that. And so when this jolt came along and . . . Well, anyway, thank God you were, who you were. You were really what I needed. Thank you so much for being what I needed.

Perhaps F understands.

F   You were what I needed too.

B   I've only fallen more and more in love with you. I'll make the quiche. But we might not have everything for the base, so it'll probably be more like an omelette. But we can still call it a quiche.

F can only smile, searching B's face.

B   You know I love you.

F   I love you too.

B   Past knowing. (*Deliberately repeating herself.*) I love you.

Beat.

F   I love you too.

B very gently pulls off F's clip-on earrings, places them in F's palm and rubs F's lobes.

They gently press their foreheads together.

At the same time:

A FINAL SWELL OF SONG –
SADNESS AND JOY TOGETHER
AS LIGHTS DIM

Printed in the USA
CPSIA information can be obtained
at www.ICGtesting.com
LVHW022102040524
779267LV00002B/373

9 781350 438835